SELECTED POEMS

NEIL POWELL

SELECTED POEMS

Some of the earlier stuff...

Nei.

CARCANET

Published in Great Britain in 1998 by
Carcanet Press Limited
4th Floor, Conavon Court
12-16 Blackfriars Street
Manchester M3 5BQ

A CIP catalogue record for this book
is available from the British Library.

ISBN 1 85754 350 5

The publisher acknowledges financial
assistance from the Arts Council of England.

Set in 10pt Garamond Simoncini by Bryan Williamson, Frome.
Printed and bound in England by SRP Ltd, Exeter.

'Dedicated to my friends pictured within'

– Edward Elgar, note on the score of
the *Enigma* Variations

Contents

III 1987-1997

I
1966-1975

Wickham Market

The smell and feel of leather fill the bar.
The farmers fake oblivion, or else stare
Resentment, looks more weatherbeaten than
The invader's crumpled armour. There the rain
Has streaked a relic of some recent battle,
Evidence that elements are more brittle
Than his shell. And yet he stands rain-scarred,
His hair is limp, and his rough cheeks are teared
From the storm still raging in his eyes:
Possessing and possessed, they half-despise
Their ambiguity, for they gleam that
Quick self-knowledge which will never let
Him be touched, though it will bid all try,
Reflecting all, a mirror to each lie –
The tragic clown. He turns towards his friend,
Buys him a drink, and laughs, sensing the end
Of the last storm is also the beginning
Of the next, that loss is in his winning.

Five Leaves Left

1

It is winter.

On a beech tree
by my window
I see five leaves hanging.

Listen to them falling.

2

The bird morning
loud then terrible
grew. And I knew

the trees had changed.

It was the bird
morning I wrote
some white word
on a wall, knowing
almost all. The word

has no meaning.

In that momentary pride,
the heart of summer died.

3

No, I am no tree. If
I were, I would have
fallen. My roots are
hacked about, and where
they still remain secure,
people stand: stay there.

4

There was always snow.

Always, slow dropping
in the receding night,
and you awoke. The world gleaming,
older now.

And colder, as time
fell thickly on the flame.

Only evening skies were red.

5

The silent sky
shone sullen through
a stained-glass window.

Light, colour, the
purple and bronze,
words cloaked deep
in gold, vague shapes
yet precise feelings.

These colours breathe
a benediction.

6

And one deeper mystery.

The cold damp evening,
the mist lingering
among the hills. No
colour, only the slow
now faster heartbeat.
Only now you forget
beat, know only that
you know.

7

The leaves fall faster
than you think. The tree
is bare. And so, later

than I had thought, am I.

And it is winter.

At Berkswell

for John & Hilary Sutton

Awaiting us, it hides, a place apart.

The village shops, the school, the almshouses
Surround it like a cold grey congregation
Who once knew how to pray, and watch in case
The place's vital essence should escape.
Proximity invites us to survey
The church's quiet order and decay.

A timbered Tudor porch stands to our right,
Incongruously welded to the flat
Substantial Norman wall: no one in sight
Except a sexton and a resident cat.
Inside, we look around, begin to know
How little changes where few people go.

Tradition too secure for sentiment
Is here encased in timber, stone, and glass,
To demonstrate that our predicament
Is unimportant. Years and tourists pass.
It waits behind here, watching us depart.
Forgetting us, it hides, a place apart.

Identities

He thinks he knows a little about love.
A river-bank, the branches crowding round,
Imprisoning the sun, the yellow leaves
Embracing, wilting slightly in the heat;
Those stream-smooth pebbles, lying just too deep
To reach. The sound of water in the hills,
A vacant summer evening closing in,
The darkening grass, the branches vanishing.
Watching his mirror-image watching him
Behind the bar, he almost loves himself.

Almost. And yet his mind is following
A cloud across a birdless winter sky,
Or prints set hard in snow, or passages
Through leafless woods. The geometric trees
Do not embrace: they touch, scratch and unfold
The wounds of winter, the futility
Of making contact. Best to stand and drink
Secure in some bright apathetic world;
To wait, and hope someone will penetrate
His abstract code, but still not understand.

It is an old accepted paradox,
Escape's vague border with reality.
He needs a bar, an image and a pose
To which the moss of solitude will cling.
He turns and says, 'The counterpoint of Bach
Is like that of the Modern Jazz Quartet
But not so brittle.' Living in an age
Of jagged noises and too brittle sounds,
We choose either the wilted summer leaf
Or else the branches' patterned skeleton.

He thinks of blind men, tries to share the lack
Of image crushed upon the retina:
They have their perfect vision, not the sight

Of years or days or placid winter skies;
Yet he retains the fading vestiges,
The summers and the fallings out of love.
He chooses winter, treading where the fox
Has trod, where rabbits ran some other day,
And where the tracks are frozen hard. He thinks
He knows too little and too much of love.

Previous Convictions

Whether it snowed much that winter is unimportant:
        it was a beginning and as such, chiefly,
I shall remember it. The bar we sat in was brown-
        painted: a gas fire spluttered irritably
in one corner, the landlord in another; Christmas
        loomed, a conventional iceberg, easily
navigated. Season of booze and Bach: each evening
        we listened to cheap records, drew from the sound
of a flautist's drastic breathing and the impatient
        scrape of furious 'cellos a deeper strand
of pleasure than from more perfect art.
                                        Or that at least
        was how it seemed, or seems now: the imperfections
necessary evidence of a humanity
        certain to disappear at any moment,
lost in the immaculate circle at the centre
        of the record. The intransigence of sound,
which at its most intimate keeps its distance, held us
        close and apart. We cannot talk of music,
we can only listen: the academic, given
        to confusing criticism with the art
it feeds on, finds in it pleasure and perplexity;
        for print does not contain it, nor notation
yield the essence of its mystery.

And, driving back
from some lonely pub, deep among the frosty
hopfields, we bounced from side to side of a steep-banked lane,
while the Irishman on the back seat hardly
stopped talking, and claimed afterwards not to have noticed.
There, buried in the night and in the country,
we devised ideas of life and friendship, to ripen
through summer and be crushed like fallen berries
in the autumn. Their stains remain, more permanent than those
of ordinary fruit.
Like grey prophecies,
multiplying smoke strata hung in that vaulted room,
long after music had ended and bottles
were empty. The sound of the rain increases slowly,
and the smoke begins to settle into dust.

Wood Farm

Clutching this twisted rusty
key, like some furtive gaoler,
I find the back door. Slowly,
the lock unsticks. I enter,
glancing quickly round although
only nettles live here now.

This place lacks the old-house smell
of rotting timber, other
autumns' leaves, and the quick fall
of crumbling plaster. I stare
across the ochre air, drawn
to interminable brown.

The beams creak; the rain gently
taps on a cracked window-pane;
and outside the falling grey
East Anglian afternoon
turns silently to evening
as I wait here wondering

about our pasts and futures.
Farmers prospered here: their food
graced this oven; their pastures,
lands made heavy with their blood,
are barren now; the soil grows
mere scrub, dead with its owners.

And dead for the future too.
Rest in peace. Let the poppies
colour this place and the dew
shine on the shattered windows,
reflecting through slow decay
a natural dignity.

A Modern Jazz Quartet

DUKE ELLINGTON

Modern? Of course: *Ulysses*
and *The Waste Land* were written
long before *Mood Indigo*.

Though at ease with a keyboard,
pen rather than piano
is your chosen instrument,

the writer's craft replacing
performer's pyrotechnics
in the study's sanctuary:

a poet, substituting
orchestra for typewriter.
I wish I knew the language.

CHARLIE PARKER

Time has distilled these moments,
has sanctified place and date:
Los Angeles, '48,

the point at which suffering
and expertise intersect
in a blues called *Parker's Mood*.

A secret, mysterious
music of purity and
uncanny classicism:

it is clearer now because
unrivalled and unsurpassed,
distilled through a sense of time.

THELONIOUS MONK

During an alto solo
at the Royal Festival Hall
you stood up and blew your nose.

The gesture was typical,
the solo was very dull,
and most of us got the point.

So, typically, you find
a perfect absurdity
in the cracks between the keys;

for reverence is no use
to a music which rejects
the gloss of solemnity.

JOHN COLTRANE

You managed the paradox:
out of certainty you brought
the music of confusion.

Through commitment you had seen
that tone does not carry truth:
one must travel in-between.

There is no perfection here
for each new cluster of notes
diminishes certainty.

One would not have guessed your creed
could be so painfully wrought
into such complexity.

Distons Lane

for Ian Smith

I'm still a stranger here. As I approach
A woman crosses to the other side,
Suspicious and afraid that I encroach
On her town's secret privacy or pride.
I understand I am not understood.

I do encroach. I see what's beautiful
In these stark cottages of yellow stone:
The bleakness and the silence of it all.
She sees a grimy terrace, cold, run-down:
A dead-end street, the dead end of the town.

She's known this town too long to be amazed
By filtered sunlight seeping to her yard:
Stone-coloured light, diffusing as she gazed
Into the bronze, stone-mellow and stone-hard.
I understand I am not understood.

She's seen some changes. Her young husband fought
In the Great War, if not the other one
Before it. Now she guards her past in thought:
The cobbles covered, all the gaslamps gone,
A dead-end street, the dead end of the town.

She passes me and glances back in fear,
A shrinking face within an old grey hood.
I smile and know I'm still a stranger here.
'It is not, nor it cannot come to good'?
I understand I am not understood.

Period Three

I stop before the door, compose myself,
Then enter slowly. Certain faces turn
To contemplate my manner or my tie;
A few glance quickly, anxious now to learn
What Wordsworth really meant, and instantly.
I look around for signs of coming storms,
And swiftly launch into the holy life
Of music and of verse and UCCA forms.

The wind is rising: halfway through Book One,
The man's done nothing but apologise
For not quite being Milton; even worse,
His idle boasts and foolish prophecies
Are fossilised in blank and turgid verse.
I answer: and the correspondent breeze
Picks up my notes and elsewhere sets them down.
I stare into the unWordsworthian trees,

And know, however dimly, I am right
To proffer in this heavy autumn room
The relevance of all those thinking things
To all these thinking people. Through the gloom
Of apathy, a voice speaks, a bell rings;
Outside the open window, others shout.
The half-extinguished visionary light
Abruptly and annoyingly goes out.

So, irritated rather than perplexed,
I gather up my notes; now from behind
A thoughtful voice asks, 'Could I have a word?'
I tell him, 'Yes, of course: what's on your mind?'
And as he speaks I realise he's heard
It all. He's not the brightest of the class,
But he has seen a poem not a text,
And understood, although he may not pass.

I wander down the corridor, my pace
Too evidently lacking urgency:
A colleague says good morning and I stare
Past him into the dark immobile sky –
That loony poet bloke. I need some air,
But steel myself to teach another bunch.
I stop before the door, prepare to face
Another forty minutes before lunch.

Afternoon Dawn

for Rod Shand

They are felling the dead elms
to the west: the sidelong sun
surprises the room after
a hundred years of shadow.
The forgotten web and dust
on untouched books are sunstruck.
Clearly, something has begun.

Things that had been unspecial
are transmogrified, reborn
to *duende* and charisma.
Sun settles on faded spines;
crystals through a decanter;
chases spiders in this, its
perversely afternoon dawn;

lights upon Márquez: *through the*
window they saw a light rain
of tiny yellow flowers
falling. Through the window I
see a blue haze of woodsmoke
spiralling towards evening,
hovering, rising again.

The room begins to darken;
now, blood-coloured light splashes
across the page where the pen
labours towards conclusion.
An end to the beginning,
the web once more unnoticed;
the elms will soon be ashes.

A Pebble

A pebble vanishes. I watch the ripples
Fatten like folds in grey concentric flesh.

The bristling reeds entangle and distort
Those outer circles. River banks enmesh

The insubstantial currents of the mind,
Whose streams contend with assonance and stress.

The poem's flow – the rock pools or the bends,
Metre or syntax, shaping its slow progress –

Becomes a formal fountain as we turn
Our private art to public artifice;

And pebbles dropping softly from a bridge
Are caught within a cave of brittle ice.

At Little Gidding

for Matthew Desmond

1

In one hand Eliot, in the other Pevsner:
And yet we have arrived here unprepared.

2

Outside the farmhouse, a removal van
Announces a more permanent arrival:
Those clean cream walls seem inappropriate;
New settlers upset the visitor.

3

But not the church, which has seen worse than this:
Scrubby bushes, grey pock-marked façade
Proclaim a calm more honest and more modest,
God's domesticity.

4

        The scale is human.
Thus, quizzically, you rightly say you find
The tombstones more impressive than the church.
Grandeur was never Nicholas Ferrar's style;
His, the potent blend of craft and creed.

5

Not that this is Nicholas Ferrar's church.
It is his spirit's church; his church's spirit
Inhabits the carved ceiling of the chancel,
Informs the space beneath.

6

                              We sign the book.
Something you had not guessed had yet begun
Is completed in this ritual: the place
Belongs to us now; we are part of it.

7

Lifesize, it will stay with us as token
Of the size a life should be: it questions,
And Pevsner's words, not Eliot's, reply,
'Little Gidding is a confusing church.'

8

Only respect transcends confusion. Yes,
In the end, we were impressed. Deliberately,
We close the door, for birds are troublesome
(A notice tells us) and this church is loved.

9

Leighton Bromswold: 'Wonderful,' says Pevsner;
But we have no taste for it today.

The Key

You offered me the key. I saw
How shrewdly it was cut, how well
The cunning craftsman knew the door
It would control: I saw it all.
You should have offered it before.

The patterns forged in steel or rock
By smith or sculptor have no grace,
Mere remnants of the solid block
Until they fill a chosen space.
You should have given me the lock.

In the Distance

First, the foreground. A class is reading,
Gratefully engrossed and undisturbed
By coughs or scraping metal chairs on wood.
Now is a time to watch unwatched, observe
The chin upon the wrist, the narrowed eyes,
The stifled yawn, the silence; and outside
An autumn bonfire flaring in the distance.

Consider this October close-up: hands
Clasped after the cold in new discovery
Of each other's throbbing warmth; a pen
Composing doodles no one understands;
A briefly broken train of thought; and then
The meditative meeting, nose with thumb.
Mist is blurring the horizon distantly.

The years are misting over. I recall
Something I didn't say a dream ago,
Return abruptly to the reading class.
The weeping condensation on a window
Becomes the image of another day,
A conversation in a different place
Minutely glimpsed, and very far away.

What casual things define me! Clothes I wear,
Books I carry, a ballpoint on the desk
Upon a half-corrected essay: there
Is all the life I seem to have. The trees
Branch from the mist, their structures become clear:
The bonfire flashes sharply as I stare
Across a hundred yards, a dozen years.

In the distance, on a Kentish hillside,
A boy is writing a poem I know by heart.

For You

31 OCTOBER 1973

A sudden solitude reveals itself
In ill-cooked meals, half-eaten; washing-up
Stacked jagged in the sink; bad sleep at night.
Or in a crowd I look around for you
As if you or your likeness could appear
Among the patchwork lights within the dark,
Among the minutes, silent and alone,
While the clock turns to a derelict November.

The grey has polarised to black and white,
The unreal clarity of an exploded view:
A local ailment blossoms to a blight –
The poverty of self-indulgence! True,
But those are all the words I'd have to write,
When all the other songs had failed, for you.

8 JANUARY 1974

Storms follow your departure: suddenly
I inhabit a community of rain.
A barn blown over, floods, a fallen tree
Map out the battered landscape. And again
Rain comes from each direction; every window
Crackles like static; the insistent blast
Rips honeysuckles from the wall as though
It means this January to be their last.

I lose myself in books as if the page
Could purge the weather or the memories
The storm has carried with it in its passage.
I think once more of other loyalties:
Letters to write, but nothing left to say.
The world had seemed much calmer yesterday.

EASTER SUNDAY 1974

The shadow of the house lies on the lawn.
The vicar walks through sunlight on the road
To evensong. I puzzle in despair:
Should I, unchristian, find redemption there
Or must I look elsewhere for resurrection?
But he has disappeared: and here's the pen,
The paper for a statement – yes, my credit,
In love as in religion, overdrawn.

31

I know that I have overplayed my hand –
Reason enough for anyone to wonder
Which was the first, the quintessential blunder?
Outside the light has dimmed insidiously;
The shadow of the house has climbed the trees.
I know that this is not the promised land.

24 APRIL 1974

For you, I leave the other words unsaid,
Or say them to myself. It's getting near,
This end, too near to distance or to dread:
Activity kills time when time breeds fear.
If once I dreamed of effortlessly reaching
The fragrant plateau, then I was deluded;
My place is in the valley, learning, teaching,
And that is where my bargains are concluded.

'Anyway, thanks,' your letter ends. It's you,
My friend, to whom the deeper thanks are due,
And those who shared our crises, lost our sleep –
The friends we keep to have and have to keep.
We may no longer prosper and deceive
The other greater world. For you I leave.

6 MAY 1974

I pay this debt of friendship willingly.
You will and it is right you never know
How long those paragraphs were in my mind.
Remember how we spoke of empathy
In someone else's world, a life ago?
That region I shall never leave behind.
The here and now afflicts me like a cramp:
I seal the envelope; I lick the stamp.

Ellington is playing: yours and yours.
The years have coalesced without a pause:
I see their fabric not their pattern now;
That and the music's languid river flow
Towards eternity. You hear it. Thus,
You know too well what will remain of us.

Going to Bed

Older, we no longer are afraid
        Of going to bed.
Listen to the cosy middle-aged:
        Ten-thirty, they tread

The worn and faded floral staircarpet,
        Clutching the banister,
Losing spectacles, spilling cocoa, asking,
        'Are you ready, dear?'

Yes, they are ready, who have traded in
        Most of their youth
For comfortable, honest indignity –
        Their kind of truth.

A style we might mock or discredit
        Too casually
Is theirs, earned by trust or by habit:
        So when I see

The ashtray and the tangle of our clothes
        Heaped on the floor,
I feel for us a touch of fear although
        We've been here before.

Suffolk Poems

JULY, 1974

Summer blossoms in fuchsias,
geraniums, hollyhocks,
and pointless casual death.
The day before I arrived,
a local man was murdered:
'following an incident
outside an hotel,' a youth,
the paper tells me, was charged.

And within the same fierce week
visitors to the Tower
of London were killed or maimed
by an unwarned explosion.
I think, above all, of friends
trapped in embattled Cyprus,
hearing only their voices
in each day's six o'clock news.

It will get worse. This is not
hopeless fear or mere despair,
but the knowledge that we grow
into deeper local grief
or international sorrow.
So, thanks to the wild east coast,
its marshes, wheatfields, relics,
all these unlikely havens.

CRAG PATH

Do the gulls pose on flagpoles, breakwaters, applauding
          others' aerobatic gestures in mirthless
dull chuckles? Or, on the beach like birds of porcelain
          perched upon a tiled suburban mantelpiece,
do some train a proprietary eye on distance,

34

less mobile than the shingle which supports them?
Here, colours usurped by the makers of paperware –
        pink, primrose, pale blue, indeterminate green –
decorate all the eccentric apparatus: steps,
        railings, shutters, balconies and verandas,
the crazy architecture where each inch of sea view
        is reason enough for structures which no child
would make in Meccano and hope to remain standing.
        Attics climb on tiled or turreted shoulders;
giddy towers rise straight-faced and lop-sided, and not one
        topples as it should into the grey North Sea.
At sunset, the couples arm in arm along Crag Path
        wander, pointing out the lifeboat, the folly,
that dear little cottage: exclamations of routine
        surprise, packaged delight, seeking no reply.
The accents – Birmingham or Edinburgh or West Ham –
        give them away. What do they see or look for,
these Pevsners of prettiness, connoisseurs of quaintness?
        For the mere detail that makes this not like home?
On the Town Steps, a solitary cat surveys them,
        off-centre, just under halfway from the top;
I respect that asymmetrical contemplation.
        It glances downwards, tucks in its paws, and yawns.

LEISTON ABBEY

Ranulf de Glanville, Robert
de Ufford, your legacies
have weathered this rough climate
half-a-dozen centuries:
more potent, more angular
than you could imagine, your

second abbey stands among
the worshipping fields of grain,
as if the North Sea had flung
its whole weight upon the plain,
leaving these crags eroded
like relics on the sea bed.

35

A meeting of ages: near
the coast the power station
eyes the chapel at Minsmere
in silent confrontation
across the marshland which shields
sanctuary among wheatfields.

IKEN

At Iken Cliff the well-fed tourists gather;
caravans, ice-cream, parodies of pleasure

drifting irresistibly towards Cliff Reach
where moody children mope at the muddy beach;

and none thinks to seek for solitude downstream
where, framed by trees, St Botolph's church awaits them,

gaunt and roofless, unthatched by fire and storm.
Decay has overtaken the postcard charm:

creepers in the tower challenge the bell-ropes;
a builder's sign recalls diminishing hopes

outside in the weed-choked churchyard. Iken lies
ruined at last after thirteen centuries,

echoes the collect for its founder: 'efface
we pray Thee the scars of our wounds and heal us.'

ORFORD

The eye with a single glance
takes in castle, church, and quay –
these emblems of endurance:
a complete community
where nothing was left to chance.

Some architect named progress
or random necessity
tamed the space from Orford Ness
to Tunstall, eternally
a fragment of Englishness.

Here is another world's end,
last haven in your journey:
trapped at a river's long bend,
eyed by castle, church, and quay –
this place the seasons defend.

LAST DAYS

When seascape becomes familiar, when you know
at what time each ship will cross the horizon
heading for which port, then it is time to go
back towards the land-locked plains of Huntingdon.

Some things defy all scrupulous inquiry,
belonging to someone else's past, giving
wrong directions, false hints, a desultory
nod and wink of secrecy. And soon, nearing

the last days of a long summer, you will scour
herbaceous borders for an opening bud
and find a drowsy bee on a late flower,
with November in your mind, frost in your blood.

Listen

Whether side-step or ascent
gets us there I hardly know:
the evening's intransigence
may be omen or portent;
objects may intrude, and no
carefully prepared defence

can protect us from them yet.
The river-mist will glisten
outside in the headlamps' gleam;
distances we must forget
are starred with cats' eyes. Listen:
the beetle nibbles the beam

and a million animals
perform their necessary
ceremonies around you
in the floorboards, ceilings, walls,
where each has his history.
Listen: how can we be true

to our world, to each other?
The nervous resolute mouse
behind the skirting is true
to hunger or cold weather
and the old warmth of a house.
Listen: the barn door swings to

and shrubs tap at the window
asking to let the world in.
To be encompassed by all
these lives and yet not to know
where to move, how to begin!
Listen: catch me as I fall.

The Way Back

Amber streetlamps punctuate the night.
Their deviously analytic glare
Reveals a world created by the light:
Not what there is but what it shows is there.

A place without surroundings: linear edge
Usurps the processes of definition
From meadowland and forest, field and hedge.
Suburban night knows only this condition,

The emptied moon's apologetic husk
Outshone by haloed sodium overhead:
Always between, always this waking dusk.
Sleep, silence, darkness: absolutes are dead.

Beyond the outskirts to the motorway:
Dark claims its spaces, but the eye moves on
Towards another imitation day –
A town or roundabout on the horizon –

Until 'The North' proclaims a giant sign,
As if the north were somewhere you could reach
By following a disembodied line
Which joins nowhere to nowhere, each to each,

And work to home. Or will it merely end
In featureless space, an orange void stretching
On each side of the road, round the next bend,
With distant amber lamps, the planets, gleaming?

Chronology

John Dankworth's clarinet, recorded
the month I was born: disconcerted,

I fumble in the shelves, discover
he was twenty-one. Turning over

the record, there's *Mop Mop*: I've that, played
by the Hawk himself, half a decade

further back. Young John and Vic don't quite
get the tricky extra half-beat right:

forgive them for youth if it inspires
these hours among the Tempos, Esquires,

Commodores, Savoys – so much to say
in each side. Old books can't talk that way.

A Spring Letter to Richard Monk

The bluebell season's over. Tattered petals
Survive among the bracken and the nettles,
Last remnants of a transitory spring
Much valued in its rapid vanishing.
The summer's brooding vigour lies in wait,
Like local thunder, claiming its estate
With armies of cow-parsley; sentries stand
On leafy guard in ceded meadowland.

Such unsurprising landscapes most surprise
By being richly there as legacies
Of other sparser seasons. Grand designs,
Mapped out by grid or megalithic lines,
Must take the details of regeneration
To be their starting-point and first foundation.
Look closer, for this latent land will yield
Worlds in a leaf, a universe in a field.

Yet at a point where those lines intersect,
In May, you have a different prospect;
At least you'd think so. My guess in this game
Is that in fact the view looks much the same
From each end of the cosmic telescope:
As long as it's in focus then there's hope.
In Somerset, in Suffolk, landscapes bring
The ages' synthesis, true summit meeting.

The difference is only of degree:
Wordsworth at Tintern, you at Glastonbury
(Leaving Leiston Abbey out of this)
Are seekers are natural synthesis –
To 'see into the heart of things', an art
More arduous than seeing to the heart
Of nothing. Thus we need a clarity
Of vision, not the mind's blind chemistry.

Pedantic or paternal? (Both, you'd say,
Believing neither.) The brash getaway
Was ever just a cover-up for fear
In those who couldn't bear to say and hear
Or wait and see: the lanes they travel through
Return, exhausted and indifferent, to
The neutral dust. Who cares for rabbits' rights
Within a world defined by wheels and lights?

All that's a shade allusive. Let's change gear
(My final – promise! – two-wheeled image here).
You'll say a hand-set, hand-sewn pamphlet's worth
Your bookshop full of Penguins: so the earth
Makes everything one-off. It's going fast,
For sure, and hard to tell if we're the last
Who'll strive to view things as they're meant to be,
Not for their use, but for their oddity.

The urge to breath some uncorrupted air,
To take a more extended trip to where
Ideas have substance strong enough to keep;
The need for some imaginative leap –
Over a stile into the bluebell wood,
Or further, elsewhere, hardly understood –
Sustains. Before we're dead we'd best be quick
But careful too. So watch the ripples, Dick.

At the Edge

Far inland this late July,
I imagine those coastlines –
Caernarvon, Sussex, Suffolk –
and think of you at the edge
of a well-studied ocean
whose dirty secrets emerge
numbered in tomato pips.

Through a vocabulary
which does what it has to do
with ungraceful exactness,
you express about the sea
things I shall never fathom,
confronting those mysteries
whose gift is their remoteness.

And yet, awed, intransigent,
I too must question; concoct
in the kitchen of ideas
the approximate flavour
of some finely-charted coast;
season it with the right words.
Scientist and writer are

not so different, perhaps . . .
Men who live on their edges,
inhabit borders, margins,
embody the coasts they crave
and need the answering clash
of waves over the shingle,
no metaphor but design.

1 August 1975

The buddleia's white-hot spears begin to rust;
A gasping sparrow staggers open-beaked
Across the flagstones; bumble bees get stuck
In sunny rooms; a year ago we met.

Time to revise love's lexicon again.
Shrub, sparrow, bee find their maturities.
Survivors struggle to the summer's brink
And celebrate in secret ceremonies.

A Cooling Universe

in memory of Matthew Desmond

1

The seasons rain on us continually,
Struck with the thunder of coincidence.
All we see of light is all we see,
Where darknesses admit no evidence
Except the final perjury of death.
Lineaments of autumn grid the page,
Flicker and jump like shadows on a hearth;
Thicken into furrows; lose their edge,
Distorting as a cloud crosses the sun,
A bird the sky, a branch the window-pane.
Conclusions signal something new begun
And histories convoked. Thus we remain
       While swallows in their purposeful migrations
       Enact the comedy of generations.

2

Enact the comedy of generations
Or else rewrite the plot; but what director
Would countenance the follies and frustrations,
The miscued lines, steps out of character
Of one predestined actor cast to choose?
Upon a littered desk the objects wait
Which have no business here but to confuse
With empty myths: old shrines we consecrate
At random visits – papers, notes and letters.
Is this the past? Redundancies of love,
Relinquished loyalties, discarded fetters:
Props too entrenched and seasoned to remove,
       Assembled as a botched-up tragedy.
       We turn their progress into history.

3

We turn their progress into history
Reversed out in a fading retrospect
By modulations to a minor key
Whose flattened thirds diminish the prospect.
Themes mingle in a child's kaleidoscope,
Distant and inexplicable, beyond reach,
In whose waking abandonment grows hope.
Music and colour surface on a beach,
Fused to a single sense: this is the way
It is when outside history and time
We see ourselves. The play becomes replay.
All sound resolves into a single chime:
       In clinging echoes, lingering vibrations,
       The air reveals its ghostly intimations.

4

The air reveals its ghostly intimations
Between last blossom and first blighted leaf:
A hinterland upon the map of seasons,
The neutral zone dividing death from grief.
Swift evening chills the amber afternoon
As, in the angles of refracted light,
The legend crystallises all too soon,
Set in relief against oncoming night.
Now in the gathering dusk where dreams begin,
The picture jigsawn into jagged parts,
We seek a frame to fit the pieces in
Or way to navigate the tangled charts:
       New islands in the mind, new continents
       Emerging in their late embodiments.

5

Emerging in their late embodiments,
The random days reconstitute a past:
We forge such fragments into monuments,
From ruins fabricate a world to last,
Composed of all the small eternities:
The breathless evenings when the mist closed in
Or embers flared in brief epiphanies
Absolving countless centuries of pain.
And thus it is the long perspective alters,
Losing itself in what envisaged it:
Facts clarify, imagination falters;
All that had seemed contained is infinite.
   Our myths will nourish us from year to year:
   They luminously glow, then disappear.

6

They luminously glow, then disappear:
It is the glancing after-light sustains
Through fractured love and superstitious fear
And what remains after the waste remains.
By charting time we find the timeless space:
The church behind the pig-sty compassing
Its infinite locality of place
Where being flowers out of visiting;
Secrets of a rainy summer wait,
Encoded, for the key which would reveal
Much to forgive and all to mitigate,
The self-inflicted wounds which will not heal.
   We come through time as suffering penitents
   Into the order of the elements.

7

Into the order of the elements,
The palsied purities of fire and ice,
We drift: impelled by endless tides and currents
Which rise as whirlpools and will not suffice
Unless to guide us to oblivion.
Death is the mother of nothing but desire
For time and energy to carry on
Against the furnace and the glacier.
A partial light illuminates these days,
Enduring although flecked with driving rains,
Chequered with leafless branches, and always
Fading: yet what thou lovest well remains.
   Dates indicate the fag-end of the year;
   At the poem's centre, meanings become clear.

8

At the poem's centre, meanings become clear:
Now (almost settled in my house) I find
The soul, still guest and not possessor here,
Hankering after something left behind.
Old tenants of this masonry persist –
Pale translucent moths which cling to beams,
Motionless for days and frail as mist,
Inhabitants of ruins or of dreams;
A single clumsy wasp; and in the grass
A resolute, self-confident bullfinch
Who seems to think that I, like time, will pass.
I claim my territory inch by inch,
   My implement a hand-trowel not a spade,
   The pattern of a world to be remade.

9

The pattern of a world to be remade
Upon the map, the same geography,
The board on which the other games were played,
Their spaces planed to domesticity:
Perhaps the mocking bullfinch understands
How scales must coexist – the sky, the nest;
How details spring from unremembered lands
Spread out below in flight – a palimpsest
Anonymous yet pregnant with the traces
Of previous encounters; homing, how
Our landmarks are the half-forgotten places
Where then entangles with the here and now;
      How, on returning, we at best may reap
      The harvest of a habitat to keep.

10

The harvest of a habitat to keep:
A safe stronghold! Such insularity!
A castle or a hole in which to creep,
Great enterprise or eccentricity?
'The writer as linguistic polymath':
Finding in Steiner this impressive phrase,
I ponder: having sought the narrow path,
Its picturesque diversions through the maze
Of learning. Gaudy plants burst into flower,
Competing in their brash proliferation:
Not Ballylee but Babel is the tower
Where blooms may thrive upon deracination.
      In avenues at evening, in the shade,
      Our legends live as they begin to fade.

11

Our legends live as they begin to fade:
Only a journal's neatly dated pages
Preserve notations, evidence displayed
To time, whose cool indifference assuages
So much that seemed in vain or hard to tell
Or merely ludicrous. This parasite
Of a blotchy past – all anecdote and libel,
Indulgences of whisky and midnight –
Still clings: a history of trivia;
A survey of decisions undecided;
An inventory of impedimenta,
Life's modest clutter, easily derided;
       And griefs for which it is too late to weep
       As time and distance beckon us to sleep.

12

As time and distance beckon us to sleep,
Lines soften in shadows. Here at least
Bleak landscape and clear light may help to keep
A style plain as the wheatfields of the East
Or other regions whose topography
Enforces its unwritten discipline –
Llano and tundra, wilderness and scree,
Where space and sparseness suddenly align.
Such landscapes should dictate a clarity
Of vision, an economy of words,
A still life rather than a tapestry:
We see the trees because there are no woods.
       Lines soften: thus for landscape and for verse
       The curtain falls on all we could rehearse.

13

The curtain falls on all we could rehearse:
The opening chords of winter's overture
Sound in the distance like a muttered curse
From ancient giant ghosts, the last of laughter.
Once the grave was merely metaphor,
Death a necessity acquitted by
Infirmity or age, where to have gone before
Proclaimed departure: the obituary
Of ancestors is written by our lives;
The autumn of the body is a season
Witnessed by every child in relatives.
Mortality evolves from myth to reason,
       The past a loan we cannot reimburse,
       Hot fragments of a cooling universe.

14

Hot fragments of a cooling universe
Survive among the glacial confusion;
A first death met on equal terms is worse
Than every other well-prepared conclusion.
Time dusts an empty stage where silver light
Lets details and delineation fade,
Sharp contrasts and reflections melt from sight.
The images of summer have decayed
Like overripened and unharvested
Blackberries rotting in an unknown lane,
Waiting for extinction's sombre tread.
Stark branches and a falling sky remain;
       The swallows and the shadows leave the tree;
       The seasons rain on us continually.

15

The seasons rain on us, continually
Enact the comedy of generations;
We turn their progress into history.
The air reveals its ghostly intimations
Emerging in their late embodiments;
They luminously glow, then disappear
Into the order of the elements
At the poem's centre. Meanings become clear:
The pattern of a world to be remade,
The harvest of a habitat to keep.
Our legends live: as they begin to fade,
As time and darkness beckon us to sleep,
        The curtain falls on all we could rehearse,
        Hot fragments of a cooling universe.

II
1976-1986

Four Quarters

NORTH

Some people and the north wind seem to wait
Round blind corners for surprised encounters.

Sunlight fractures in the brittle air,
Dazzles from redundant puddles, windows,

And in odd angles of contorted trees.
Iron twigs litter the ground; milk-bottle tops

Scuttle along the streets; the morning breathes
An amazed gasp of adversity, of life.

EAST

Snow grits the earth like dusty splinterings
Of a distant frozen planet breaking up.

Some granulated arctic mineral,
Sprinkled from a cosmic pepper pot,

Garnishes with winter's condiment
The nervous spring's uncertain vegetation.

Sheer pretence! The pavement reasserts
Its wet grey mastery at every step.

SOUTH

Insomnia on a sweaty April night:
Shades of sirocco in North Hertfordshire.

Wizened old stems of an hibiscus sprout
Anaemic and unprecedented shoots

As if put out, as I am, by the warmth
Of a transparent suffocating blanket

Gently settling on the universe,
Breezing away the dominion of the air.

WEST

The west wind stiffens as the rain comes on.
The church tower vanishes into stone sky.

Blossoms enact unseasonable autumn,
Flutter across a screen of monochrome.

The sound of distant traffic conjures up
Wet homeward journeys on forgotten roads.

Past and future dance outside the window,
Rejoicing in the end of a dry season.

The Bridge

One stands above an upstream cutwater,
Rod angled aimlessly towards the land,
Safe in his niche; while on the other side
His friend leans on the opposite pilaster,
Arms braced against the stone and legs astride
As if to clasp the bridge with either hand.

There are no fish. The first knows this and smiles:
It is enough to be a part of air
And sun and stone and water, bridging them.
His line into the river runs for miles,
Transfigured from the rod's initial stem
Into the web of currents everywhere.

His friend feels none of that. He stares downstream
Where sunlight catches an abandoned tyre
And glances back in glossy insolence,
Hardened into a rigid silver gleam.
The clasp upon the parapet grows more tense.
Sweat chills his neck. The stonework is on fire.

Between the bridge's piers the river brings
Its casual luggage and its fluent art
Past those whom it will neither curse nor bless:
One is detached because a part of things,
The other restless in his separateness.
The bridge which bears them carries them apart.

The Other Night

I dreamt of you the other night. It seems
The fractured days reticulate my dreams.

First there were the retrospects, the glances
At real events and places, hopes and chances,

From which I woke to the anaemic glow
Outside the clarifying dawn window,

Pretending 'I knew it couldn't be' – and still
In time I learnt to dream that codicil.

So, the other night, I must have cried,
'It can't be – it's a dream'; but you replied,

'It's not, it's real: the other was the dream.'
Convinced, I tried to comprehend the scheme,

Only to wake: the same walls, the same ceiling.
Soon I shall learn to dream the reawakening.

Does this mean I shall wake among the dead?
Memories unwind inside my head.

Somewhere

Logs are being sawn somewhere:
Easing through the softened air,

Heavy with rain and sodden leaves,
The sound of blade on timber gives

An edge to cloud's infinities.
Mist buttresses the nervous trees,

Smoke jostles where the cloud resists,
But there below the saw persists.

The blade gives edge to what it takes.
The world is split. The timber breaks.

Sur la Terrasse

a painting by David Hockney

Limits: distance and near edge.
Here you are contained, and yet
hills and trees delineate
a further world. The curtains
know their place and hesitate,
held back, restrained: open doors
are the best we can hope for.

But listen. Don't turn. There is
another distance within
where the eye shapes, translating
image into imagery:
beyond the curtains, casting
a separate glance and now
a shadow within shadow.

Being and seeing are more
than the best we could hope for:
now all the generous light
is yours. On the terrace you
keep distance and edge in sight
and are them, contained: see how
the shadows bend towards you.

A Season of Calm Weather

1. A MOSSY WALL IN SIDGWICK AVENUE

Random, the resurfacing of pain:
A mossy wall in Sidgwick Avenue
And, on the path, familiar slur of leaves . . .

Why should this bite? Why should it, come to that,
Conjure a false familiarity
In one by choice unCantabrigian?

Such pangs are symptoms of uncharted loss,
Snapshots of another, fictive life
Brought quickly into focus, brightly lit.

Resurfacing of pain: bringing to light.
Yet, not to evade a small semantic tangle,
Resurfacing a path is covering up.

To cover up the pain I kick the leaves
Which covered up the path, resurfacing
A little of the random world, like rain.

2. BEYOND MY MEANS

I gather that I live beyond my means.
'DR,' the statement stutters: short for 'drat',
I'd like to think, or maybe even 'drunk'.

No such luck: the message, clear enough,
Is more-diluted special-offer scotch,
The twelve-year-old malt banished to the past.

Outside, the mortgaged world is freezing hard,
And I at last ironically a 'member'
Of a Building Society! Will it help or matter

That this one has a poet on its board?
By all accounts, our poems will be worth
As little as our love, less than our shares.

3. AFTERMATH

'I heard the Stones at Madison Square,' you said,
Shyly. I liked that. After all the fuss
The others made at Knebworth for the Floyd,

For 'festivals' on bogged-down, windswept fields,
Reluctant understatement stopped them dead.
Where did you learn to try not to impress?

4. NORTH HERTFORDSHIRE

Pesthouse Lane, Dead Street, and Limekiln Lane
Are Clothall Road, Queen Street, and Kingsland Way:
The Ministry of Truth's at work again.

Strange, this desire to cover up the past,
Its plain style of abrasive honesty,
As if the past might give too much away.

In Pepper Alley, off the Market Place
(The name no doubt retained through oversight),
Spices were sold; here cautious windows peep

With sidelong glances down high walls inscribed
'Lincoln Boot Boys', 'Blacks Out', 'Spurs OK'.
What's happened to the language of the tribe?

5. AT BALDOCK

Silas Howes, Swan Brand, and Plummer Craft,
Their names and times Dickensian, reproach
Incurious passers-by, late daffodils.

Emboldened letters, weather-eaten words
Outstare a hundred years to tell us all
Their widows thought that we should know of them.

'Wife of the above': things said, unsaid.
A century of winters keeps intact
Relationships, degrees, each in his place.

'Thomas Rodd, of London.' Far away:
A place to be of, come from, ending here
Beneath brave stones in foreign Hertfordshire.

6. A SLEEVENOTE ON THE GOLDBERG VARIATIONS

To earn a footnote in some history;
To slide through time, like Goldberg, by mistake;
To gain a niggling notoriety . . .

These are the gentler and the nobler fames,
Distinguished by their pure contingency,
Their guileless innocence of clever games

And ways to make a splash. We cannot choose
The resonances which attach to names,
Nor can we, thus immortalised, refuse

To designate a rose or dead-end street;
A set of variations or a blues;
A plain stone or an ornamental seat

Inscribed 'In memory of' beside a lake;
A square, a hall, a place where people meet
And take our names in earnest, by mistake.

I walk through the silent town. A breeze is blowing
Snuffed-out candles from horse-chestnut trees.
The unknown is on the air, and I am knowing

Something I cannot recognise, unless
It is a distant prospect of the future, showing
All that is and all that will come to be,

As blossoms of the past are going, going.

The Last Field

In the last field he would pause before the stile,
Look back across the furrowed ploughland, know
The lineaments of landscape as his own:
Time-softened hillsides; fences overgrown;
The muddy lower fields; the lusher meadow;
A dog-legged footpath limping mile on mile.

And always, here, an image: one weekend,
Home from school for half-term in November,
He had surveyed this huddled group – the spire,
The farmhouse and the ragstone barns – and higher,
Held in the charcoal sky, a single ember,
The swollen smouldering sun, poised to descend.

He watched until the barns eclipsed it, then
Stood motionless in gathered dusk and mist:
Land taking texture from the ragstone walls,
Hardening, darkening in the slow withdrawals
Of colour, light, and clarity. At last,
He turned towards his homeward path again.

He crossed the stile and wandered on, his task
To draw his mind from the encroaching land.
The image lingered as it lingers still:
Thus, following the dog's leg path downhill,
I scan the ragged skyline as I stand
Before the stile, forging a homeward mask.

Days

Some days promise well. Refracted sun,
Cut by others' glass, enlightens mine;
The curtains warm where, luminous as wine,
Light seeps between the ended and begun;
At last the shapes of midnight disarray
Are redrawn in the brittle lines of day.

Already clouds obstruct the common light:
The gleam has gone – we missed it once again
And now the world seems, as it is, mundane.
Orange juice, toast, coffee, the quick bite
For breakfast and the newspaper's quick read:
Each satisfies a habit, not a need.

And the edenic dawn? No more than rest
Doing its job, easing us through its phase
Of waking optimism. What are days
But different ways of failing, or at best
Of seeming to succeed? How well we seem,
Depending on the state of mind or dream,

Will not in fact reveal how well we are.
The morning folds; the afternoon spreads out
Its greying manifesto; care and doubt
Thicken in the unconditioned air.
Slowed and dyspeptic after lunch, we find
Surrounding us the dull lethargic grind

Which trades as working, earning, getting on.
Words fail like slabs to pave our arguments
While elsewhere, naggingly, the mind presents
An image of . . . it could be anyone,
Through all the sad delusions, all the pain,
Going downhill, alone, into the rain.

With the Sea

1

At Dunwich you feel like a trespasser on the earth:
          on sunken paths through the mushroom-scented wood
past the last monastery wall and the last gravestone
          (John Brinkley Easey, uneasy at the brink)
to the cliffs' edge and the last church tower out at sea.
          They say the bells still peal, perhaps to restore
some tenuous hope of immortality, while bones
          gesture a final desultory farewell.

Trespasser? Tenant? Neither will win, the sea insists,
          in the vanished places – Dunwich, Walberswick –
where lanes scrawl to the margin of a torn-off coastline
          whose history is rewritten by the tide.
Think, the sea persists, of your monuments and cities,
          skills and crafts, in the scale of natural time;
and then remember eleven Dunwich churches drowned
          off this temporary coast; tread carefully.

Too simple to wish a lingering death concluded:
        'the halo of traditionary splendour'
(the Reverend Alfred Suckling, 1848)
        still glimmers here in the wasted vacancy.
A scything north-easterly wind, sleet across the sea,
        and a burdened sky weigh down upon the land:
trespasser, tenant, artist, walk tentatively here,
        your world undercut by erosive waters.

2

        And all of us seek transactions with the sea.
Permanently shifting, it is the permanent force
        in our shifting lives; so we edge to the coast,
the quiet stony beach, the silted estuary,
        knowing what to expect and finding surprise,
a new light reflected across familiar water.
        And thus our returns, if not always happy,
are at any rate truthful: bright redefinitions
        of our place in life, with the sea insisting
on its right as the source of our selves and our emblems.
        The dogs bringing driftwood, patient retrievers,
seem to hint at some need in the human condition;
        kids skimming pebbles, encamped night fishermen
are celebrants too of a secret communion;
        bather and sailor, artist and craftsman share
epiphanies: as through the sea-mist, discovered sun
        lights upon the suddenly envisioned waves.

Out of Time

I come to you again
Across the years; across
The miles of poppies, gorse,
And tattered villages;
Across the line between
The Midlands and the East
Where land gives way to sky;
Across the Suffolk plain.

Walking along the shore
Beneath the mallowed wall
To the Martello tower,
Knowing these limits now,
These shifting constancies
Of tides and boundaries,
At last I learn the pace
I should have learnt before.

My prison is the sea:
You rule my movements now
And make me move with you.
I come here willingly
Yet when I go, I go
Against my will and yours.
You liberate, enclose:
My prison sets me free.

I hear this song once more
After a dozen years:
Unnerving synthesis
Of timelessness and time.
Chris Farlowe sings it still
On a juke-box in the pub –
Summer of '66,
The future all in store –

Time-capsule of a song!
This continuity
Of shingle and of sea,
Past-self and future-self,
As faded summers flare
In a song across a bar,
Reminds me that I've 'been
Away for much too long'.

A dozen years have passed
Since I paced out this shore,
Full of unripened plans
Of all there was to be done:
Of all I could have done
In a dozen empty years!
I should have stayed at first.
I shall remain at last.

Windows

First and best is a window to the sea
When homing fishing-boats are silhouettes
As early sunlight tints the empty beach;
Or when, past shadowed shingle, water glows
In slow dusk and the flecking lighthouse-beam
With triple gesture comforts, charms and warns.

The second window opens onto plains
Where wheatfields stretch from nearby ear and stem
Until the stared-at skyline disappears.
In winter, stripped, the earth reveals itself:
Its muscular and bleak topography
Teaches endurance, promises rebirth.

Third and last is a window onto trees.
It will do for now: I like this filtered light.
The willow dusts the grass; the copper beech
Has weathered its long autumn gracefully;
And soon, when leafless branches web the sky,
The trees will show new lines, lucidities.

Stages

for Ben Staines and Tim Watson

THE PROLOGUE

He's part of the scene. He gestures
Disdainfully towards action,
Outlines a map on which honour
And dishonour form the contours.

He's above such paltry matters
As treachery, loyalty, love:
The deaths of fools and princes
Are ancient history to him.

He apologises slyly
For his world's deficiencies:
You will kindly imagine
An army, a fight now and then.

He's on your side really:
He hopes you won't heckle
Or insist on a refund,
Yet he doesn't trust actors.

He won't go away. He belongs.
At home you'll discover him
Washing up, gardening,
Cooking: part of the scene.

THE TENT

Again they call. They pester, and I grow
Hour by hour more obdurate – 'obtuse'
The prissy politicians say – although
Ulysses must know why I refuse
His eloquent requests. Not vanity
But strength with which he justly credits me
Insists that I pursue the life I choose
And counteracts his cool diplomacy.

They use more language than they understand:
Their schoolboy honour is a travesty
To make a childish scrap in no-man's land
Into a battle fought for king and country.
This silly prank is Menelaus' game –
His bitchy wife, his folly, and his shame.
Chucking him was sense, not destiny:
If I'd been Helen I'd have done the same.

And yet we came and did our best to please,
Playing by their rules. 'Splendid,' they said.
'Don't stop: your reputation tarnishes
Unless you keep it polished till you're dead.'
Their honour comes with that persuasive catch,
A built-in bribe to keep you up to scratch:
One false move, and honour's disappeared,
For who recalls the star of last year's match?

But life and sport are really not the same
(They'd find the difference inconvenient).
When I'm a corpse I'll have no taste for fame;
Till then, my taste demands life's nourishment:
Food, drink, and love are all that's precious.
Again they call. What will become of us?
They speculate and sneer at our intent.
Let Agamemnon stew. More wine, Patroclus.

A DEATH

The day recedes. Blood floods across the plain.
There suddenly is nothing left to say,
Nothing to do but turn around again.
You should have known that it would end this way.

Now what you could not do is done at last –
'Achilles hath the mighty Hector slain' –
And what you could not be is in the dust
Behind your horse. Your triumph is in vain.

A hero for a corpse is poor exchange
On either side, and this especially,
Of all beautiful losers. And that's strange:
For he now is what you feel you should be,

As legend crystallises from his past.
You watch the clinging failure of your schemes:
You drove a bargain too hard and too fast,
And sheltered kids grow up to have bad dreams.

A DREAM

In a dream I wake within the empty space:
There must be someone in this cold dark place.

In a dream the lights are out, the doors are locked,
The entrances and exits are all blocked.

In a dream the flats collapse, the rostra split:
Battlements litter the abandoned set.

But when did everybody disappear?
Why did the actors go and leave me here?

In a dream at last I reach the bedside light
Which makes dreams worse: which makes them infinite.

GIVE ME SOME LIGHT

I think I begin to get the hang of this:
'Cue thirty it is, according to my text.
Do we agree? Yes I want everything,
The whole damn lot. It's *meant* to dazzle them.'

At 2 a.m. there'll be the three of us,
Learning the hard-won intimacy that comes
From working through our breaking points. 'I've spent
Sixteen hours on this fucking set today.'

So's he, and he. It's a complicity
We share, this special energy we know
Is given only for a certain time
To recreate the truth: the play's the thing.

Or so for the time being we'll pretend.
A week from now we'll be ourselves again,
But when tomorrow night the king cries out
'Give me some light!' we'll give him all we've got.

SOLILOQUY

I listen to you speak, hear only tone;
I feel the weight of words, not what they mean.
And this seems strange, in words so used and known,
But is (I know not *seems*) not strange at all:
For words are shadows which we move between
From light to light where heavily they fall.
You do not speak thus when we are alone.

I watch you ageing, see you only young.
The world, unweeded, grows from flower to seed,
To ripe and rot; yet here upon the stage
The time is broken, out of joint indeed:
For years are prisms which we move among,
Casting their fractured light from age to age . . .
'But break my heart, for I must hold my tongue.'

WOE OR WONDER

It's our last night. Out front, I think of you,
Your calm hand restless on the cue-light switch,
Remembering our first night: a circuit blew
And left you guessing, cueless, in the dark.

The lightning storms among the battlements,
Flickers across the auditorium.
Backstage, beyond the wild and whirling words,
You make things work. The players come and go

Where we have placed them, more or less, and so
The evening gathers its contained momentum.
I watch, you hear: we're both spectators now
As this frail wooden O spins on until . . .

The rest is silence. Darkness will descend,
And all for this? 'What is it you would see?
If aught of woe or wonder, cease your search':
For what we judge, are judged by, is the end.

Solstice

December sun takes aim across the trees;
            Time pauses here;
Light finds among the boughs' interstices
            A rested year.

'So hallowed and so gracious is the time . . .'
            The shadows run
Along the winter's stage in silent mime:
            Things lost, begun.

Acts of Faith

CRABBE AT ALDEBURGH

The saltmaster's son returned. Half qualified,
Half-dreamer, half in love, and out of luck.
'Mask-*ill* – Mask-*ill*; and so you shall find me,'
Roared his employer when called by Crabbe 'Maskwell'.
But the new young 'doctor' found small employment,
His head full of botany, poetry, Miss Elmy.

Yet he remained, drawn to the protestant coast,
The poor quay at Slaughden, the splintered buildings.
1st of January 1779:
'Eleven houses here were at once demolished . . .
He saw the breakers dash over the roofs,
Curl around the walls . . . crush all to ruin.'

1780, London: 'the miserable year,'
Says the biographer son, 'that he spent in the City . . .
Nothing but disappointments and repulses.'
Crabbe's Journal, though, is brightly alert,
His patience rewarded by Burke's benevolence –
One hundred pounds – and then by Holy Orders.

So the saltmaster's son returned to the mean town,
'A man of acknowledged talents; a successful
Author . . . and a clergyman.' His feelings 'may
Easily be imagined'; and so may his welcome.
'Unkindly received . . . I had too much indignation
To care,' he admitted, 'what they thought of me.'

Embittered, he stayed only months as curate; thence,
To uneasy luxury as Chaplain at Belvoir.
It is the poems which betray him in their clear
Sight and sound of a coast you cannot leave,
The abrasive edge of solitude, for 'there
A sadness mixes with all I see or hear.'

74

HAWKER AT MORWENSTOW

for Steve Goard

East Anglia, North Cornwall . . . peninsulaic:
Regions which lead nowhere but the sea.
And he was drawn to water more than most:
To Morwenstow, by birth, by destiny,
A craggy battlefield for soul and ship,
And every wreck's embodiment a ghost.

Caught between sense and spirit! What he saw
Buckles his words and surfaces instead
In beached emblems: the *Caledonia*'s
White figurehead, 'the relique of the storm',
Over her captain's grave; above the cliff,
Hawker's hut, trained on the waves and weathers.

'Again startled! "A woman Sir, has brought
A man's right foot"'; 'A mangled seaman's heart';
'In every gust . . . a dying sailor's cry';
Charted by disaster, the years passed,
Chequered with faces like the *Alonzo*'s crew –
Their 'expression of reluctant agony'.

Unburied names: *Phoenix, Caledonia,*
Margaret Quayle, Alonzo, Avonmore . . .
'God is angry with this land,' he said,
'And so I think and fear.' His fears became
Both mask and habit, fracturing with time,
Flaking beneath 'the weather of suicide'.

No doubt he was mad at last, 'so racked and strained'
By ceaseless defeated labour. Then came ghosts.
'They thrill like an echo,' he wrote of them; 'no sound
But the words are felt all through.' Voice of the sea,
And pledge of Hawker's immortality:
'I would not be forgotten in this land.'

Coda

Thelonious Monk, d. 17 February 1982

Goat-bearded, crazy-hatted old wrong-noter:
Your half-tones filled the gaps of adolescence,
When all brave young aficionados claimed
To know what you were up to: shameless bluff,
Until one day we woke to find it true.

Thus now hands, aimless on a keyboard, fall
Into 'Round Midnight' – haunted, audible
Through the sizzling of a Riverside EP
Those twenty years ago, the sheet music
Ordered from a baffled small-town shop:

Both still possessed, with later images
Of one March night in London, '65,
Prancing before a South Bank audience.
Within the pauses and abrasive chords,
Misterioso – hermit or buffoon?

No need to choose. I couldn't understand
Then how defences crowd about the self;
How, hedged around with paradox, we lose
The centre we defend; so couldn't know
Why you fragmented sentimental songs,

Invented notes for dislocated moods,
Evaded easy treasonable concord.
I'd hope but daren't believe at last you rest,
Beyond our life's perverse cacophony,
If not in peace, at least in harmony.

Studies

for John Boumphrey

1. PARK GRANGE

A dimly disinfected corridor
Leads back into the past, through ember light
From old bulbs nested in red plastic shades.
Its intersections tempt with dark dead ends:
Cracked and clattered pantry, endless cellar,
Deep cupboards housing colonies of shoes.
There's no escape nor whimsical detour.
The furniture of fear. The silent door.

2. THE MEWS

Trust's emblems: open doors, plain *Seniors*,
Freedom of uncharted bookshelves – this
Was all the world I wished to grow into.
Up skeletal boxed stairs to attic rooms
Where adolescent literati met
And unregarded age hung in the eaves:
Contained or cobwebbed by indifference,
We traded in our different innocence.

3. THE WELL COTTAGE

The six bells tumbled over misty elms
To summon the devout, unnoticing
A grey cat in the hedge, a dew-lit web,
And a boy behind the leaded window, writing
At this desk, studious in another house.
I see him now, and want to say, 'Don't worry,
The years will heal your broken images.'
The whirligig of time brings his revenges.

4. KENILWORTH ROAD

A midland window framed another view:
Suburban trees, back gardens, washing-lines
And afternoon sun sliced by venetian blinds.
Books, records, papers tried to lend a name
To stateless furniture: identities
Lodged tentatively in a no-man's land.
The sudden warmth of strangers: good to find
Such kindness shown to one not of their kind.

5. EASTNOR GROVE

An attic in a tall and silent house,
The wrong end of town, defining solitude:
I lived, consoled by anonymity,
For six safe months – deliberate prelude
To garret life, I thought. Enough of that:
Long evenings in the Roebuck; coming of age;
A few friends in the hazy rooms; below,
The trees in Eastnor Grove were hunched with snow.

6. NEW STREET

The streetlamps flickered out in Distons Lane.
Above the arch, we played our dangerous game
Through smoky nights and aimless faded days,
Watching our selves or the receding room,
Booklined, Cotswold-stoned. It seemed enough:
Talk, music, whisky, dope, a little art,
Steps echoing in the archway; high above,
He said something or other about love.

7. THE TOWN

A hamlet called The Town. And Matthew said,
'If I lived in a place like this, I'd write.'
We crossed the river meadows from the Crown,
Returning homeward through the mellow night,
Then talked on in the open-windowed room
Where honeysuckle weighed upon the air;
Knew nothing of the imminence of loss,
An accidental end, time's double-cross.

8. CAMBRIDGE HOUSE

Suddenly space: high ceilings and white walls.
Perhaps I thought a change would set me right –
Simple as that. False logic of façades,
An each-way bet, a love at second sight,
The liar's self-conviction of a truth:
Thus caution tempts desire to leasehold life.
Bland architectural graces, signs misread:
Within, some space stayed uninhabited.

9. CHURCH STREET

Now darkness has closed in around the desk.
The night's surviving colonists stand guard –
An angled lamp and a low-glowing fire
Where random bricks are blackened by old smoke.
Scotch, coffee, and the final Brandenburg:
At last a little time belongs to us.
Outside, the street is sobered, still: it's late;
The house's timbers gently ruminate.

Listening to Rain

*'How often have I lain beneath rain on a strange roof,
thinking of home.'* – William Faulkner, *As I Lay Dying*

There were nights I'd lie awake, listening to rain
Shuddering on slates or tickling the gutter:
Nights when the universe was rain-defined,
Gaps padded with moisture, and the space
Between here and there confined within a shower.
Nearby cars were slurring round a corner
On the road home: I'd think of warm interiors,
Green glow of dashboards, air soft with tobacco,
Relaxed hands on wheels, and desultory chatter
Of those who know they'll get to where they're going.

So, there were nights: and even now I'd feel
Abrupt chilled air of a winter dormitory,
Sash windows open, curtainless, bare floor,
An iron bedstead's knotty skeleton.
Fitzgerald said it's always three o'clock
In the dark night of the soul; for me it was
Round midnight, which bewitching time intrudes,
My friend, on different myths – truncated times
Snatched from us on wet garden city streets,
Or gusty emotions in the empty early hours.

Now raindrops on a skylight merge, diverge,
Form tributaries towards the imminent sea
Which in some sunny elsewhere you're beyond:
On Rhodes it seems it's 32°,
And that at least's unenvied; while outside,
The space expands to claim a galaxy,
Inhuman and unbridgeable, where lights,
Flickering on a further shore, are doused
By absences, departures, nights I've lain
Beneath a strange roof, listening to rain.

Coming to Light

They're faint at first, watermarks
in grey antique laid paper,
apparent indentations
in the fabric of the air;

then, gently liberated
from river-mist, they reveal
themselves as masts, truncated
by harbour or by sea-wall;

and strangely, as detail grows,
the newly-defined appear
less real – dull purplish mallows
turn luminous, and the near

masts are hardening to black
snappable twigs, transient,
about to shatter or crack.
What's well lit is too present:

it's others, coming to light,
contain both future and past,
held at the limits of sight,
claimed by and claiming the mist.

North Sea Nights

1

The last of sunlight lingers on the waves,
But suddenly the sea's not sociable:
The crowds have gone; it clears up after them,
Licks picnic remnants with a surly tongue,
Erodes their little moated monuments,
And scrambles all their sandy messages.
It dumps some salty oddments in exchange:
A bargain far from rich yet more than strange.

2

He comes in looking like the past he is.
Hello. We met before. Of course. A drink.
The jukebox plays the theme from something: strings
And soapy clarinet. 'I'm here all week –
The place I always stay when I'm this way.'
We share some snatched complicity, yet know
That after-closing-time will find me home,
Black coffee, the *Times* crossword, and alone.

3

'The Mass Orgie Shelter': so it's claimed
Below the coastguard station. Not tonight:
The entertainment's vanished under cover;
Puddles recall the high tide's hangover;
Misshapen Coke cans clog the gullies; light
Sweeps out from Orford Ness; while inland, high,
Five even-spaced red military lamps
Map out another world, scarring the sky.

4

'We're from Hemel.' Tattoos say he's Tony,
While she, not so announced, remains unnamed.
They're watchful, clear-eyed. 'They must do all right
Here,' he says, 'giving such short measure.' 'No,
Rather the reverse.' 'So that's it. Oh.'
'Try buying crisps or cigarettes, you'd find
They've "just sold out": it's always like that, yet
The place has something.' Yes. We drink to that.

5

Calm tonight: a footpath on the sea
To apricot moon, a little bruised, like me.

Therfield

We sit outside, as dusk falls, with our beers.
Mine tastes autumnal: mist and smoke unfold
On cue from gardens round the village green
And shadowed lanes. The summer has grown old.

We watch the long perspective – walls and hedges
End in a distant gable – and imagine
How there we might inhabit quiet lives.
I dare not say you have no place in mine.

Visiting

Those houses are too square, those roads too straight,
And the trees, though old, look planted to conceal
Some sheltered institution – hospital
Or army base. We find the visitors' gate:
A car-park conifered as a cemetery,
Well-ordered, clean. You'd know it miles away.

Now, like all guilty secrets, it unmasks
Its human face: a shabby hall set out
With coffee, tea, as for a village fete;
Familiar transactions, social tasks
In a world removed from all we could transact;
And people round us trying to connect

The outside past – 'Do you remember?' – to this,
The present, inside. Lives have raced ahead
On different tracks, with so much left unsaid,
And now unsayable, that we dismiss
The normal words: gossip, solemnity
Seem to affront the occasion equally.

'It won't be long.' The parting sounds inane.
'We'd better let you out,' the warders smile:
The trees, of course, were planted to console.
They fail. The landscape opens once again –
A low green wood, shut pubs, a water tower –
And freedom, if that is what this is, tastes sour.

Distant Music

Across hot roofs and unfamiliar streets
Comes distant music: honed by stone and slates
Into angular shapes, it pulses, demanding
Allegiance. The piper, unpied, unyielding,
Stands on a wide white balcony, beyond
The dry contingent thoroughfare: around
This corner, up these narrow steps, and on
Through blistered high-walled alleys where the sun
Dips warily and only at midday.

The sound commands; the listeners obey.

At last, beyond the railings he is there,
In faded denim, faded yellow hair,
Charming the alto sax whose gold has won
The modest light and claimed it for its own.
It utters now an endless twining riff
That Charlie Parker played, glinting as if
The sound were light refracted and elsewhere
Returned to what it was, a part of air.

The boy has paused for breath: he stares, intent,
Perplexed and rueful, at his instrument,
As if he knows his ariel charm must vanish
Or that he too, out on the street, will tarnish.

True Colours

Today the sea is the colour of the sky,
And neither is blue. But look, at the water's edge,
There's a girl in a blossoming yellow anorak;
By her, an ultramarine man. She is the colour
Of a plausible buttercup, and he . . .
                                            They are watching,
Attentively following something I cannot see,
Until at last a sudden tiny child
Springs, as it seems, from the shingle in the drizzle,
Clutching an orange polygon.
                                    Impossibly,
The kite flies, darts like a drunk insect, crashes
Abruptly onto an astonished patchwork dog.
A matching gull flaps by, huge, out of scale.

Or so, surely, it was. For, turning again
To the rainswept window, I find that they
Have all moved out of frame. All that remain
Are the true colours: mutual, neutral grey.

III

1987-1997

Sun Street

1

A boy walks past. He's wearing faded jeans
And a garish big-checked peppermint-green shirt.
The clash is vivid and familiar:
You wore, a dozen years ago, the same
Woeful mix. I thought you colour-blind,
Or maybe just revered your recklessness;
But that was in another summer, and
Mortality is standing in the way.

2

'All right, all right,' he drawls as he walks away.
He looks like something out of *My Beautiful Laundrette*.
'You bastard,' she yells. 'I'll kill you.' 'All right, all right.'
Milk bottles smash. A child screams. And a dog,
Parked in an expensive car, yaps plaintively.

I was brooding on some niggling misery
When that little scene occurred to cheer me up.
Catharsis is too grand a word for it:
Just good to know that frustration, anger, pain
Aren't exclusively owned. On the absurd chimney
Above the butcher's shop, a blackbird calls curfew.

An Alternative Ending

for Ian Sizeland

Outside, on the veranda, chairs and table,
Their white paint pimpled by autumnal rust:
Two glasses and a cracked decanter proffer
A static invitation, an old trust.

Here change is texture and decay is growth:
The boards no longer creak, a fine silt seals
These soft interstices whose grains play host
To tawny mosses; every plank conceals

Communities of woodlice. At the edge,
A deckchair's frame surveys the wilderness
Of reedy water, tattered canvas flags,
Loose pages of the *Eastern Daily Press*;

And late sun seeps to the veranda, where
It lights, like the bright future, on a chair.

The Difference

for Adam Johnson

We watch the gathering sea through sepia dusk
Across a beach of fish-heads, glass beads, relics
Dumped by a careless deity called chance.
Ferry and trawler exchange a passing glance.

Dark comes fast: lighthouse and streetlamp pierce it.
You sit at the window, silent as I write.
We are no longer locked in self-defence.
Being with you has made all the difference.

The Lunatics' Compartment

A Courtly Epistle for A.J.

It's England, nineteen-eighty-eight.
The rain comes on, the train comes late.
I choose the lunatics' compartment:
In front a snow-thatched don, intent
On squinting back across his seat;
Behind, protruding trainered feet,
A stoned recumbent boy, half-dressed,
Prompts academic interest.

At Finsbury Park, the spiral stairs
Are urinous as ever: there's
The rumble of the train I've missed;
Two Irishmen, already pissed,
Dispute the time. Three stations on,
A grinning beefy lad gets on:
His left leg pressed on my right, he
Checks out desire's seismology.

Next into Thresher's at Earl's Court,
Seeking the dry white I'd want brought
To my own party. Outside, it's
Time to give thanks for leather jackets:
I sprint off down the rain-surged street,
Pass John Heath-Stubbs and know we'll meet
In Redcliffe Gardens, think about
Just one in the Coleherne? Better not.

Inside the hall, we greet and kiss.
You say, 'We don't usually do this
When we meet in London.' And that's so,
But here it's suddenly as though
We're self-enclosed if not alone.
A naked boy is on the phone,
And from an open door drift through
Camp music and a voice or two.

The room's embalmed from nineteen-ten:
Old furniture, old books, old men,
And now an odd perception, which is
Candles here have dimmer switches.
The wine is white and warm and sweet,
The chatter joylessly discreet;
No intellectual risks are taken
Until . . . of course, it's Eddie Linden.

Enters mid-sentence, going on
About getting mugged in Paddington,
Which makes him now, amazingly,
Sober and plastered, as if he
Is London: walking-wounded place
Whose gracefulness is in disgrace,
Whose refugees are gathered here,
The brave and literate and queer.

The naked boy, now dressed, is an
Escapee from the Barbican:
He looks around this courtly scene,
Unsure but every inch a queen,
Creating little waves of truth
As each of us recalls his youth
Or wonders who will take the plunge
And make some sad nostalgic lunge.

Elsewhere Hugh David talks about
The English Gentleman, that lout
On whom he's writing; Francis King
Decides to tango, though nothing
Seems (luckily) to come of it;
And I remember Michael Schmidt
At Earl's Court Square: 'We're getting old:
You've grown eyebrows, I've gone bald.'

It's not my scene, I guess, and so
At ten o'clock I turn to go:
I used as my excuse a train,

Though feel the pull of bars and rain.
A cinematic staircase kiss
Brings its lovely echo, this:
The poem, not our love, is finished;
I would not have that love diminished.

Creativity Essential

I'm starting to forget my friends.
I'll always remember, I'd say,
To some Mark or Rick or Gary,
Boys name-tagged like Levis.
But these days I only recall
The half-smoked joints, the tears,
Exits at 3 a.m.

It's the poems that remain:
Long autumn afternoons
With Alan arguing
About *The Sense of Movement*.
He'd lend me his books, inside
Were postcards for signposts:
'You should look at R. Fuller';
'What is C. Tomlinson up to?'

Alvarez' amoeba-covered
The New Poetry had done it.
Inside, at 'On the Move',
I'd used as bookmark another
Postcard: 'You are invited
To join The Poets Group
For the new sessions.
Creativity essential.
First meeting Tuesday 12th
October. Circa 7.30.'

Creativity essential!
(Isn't it, though!) And just what is
This creativity?
If you find out, let me know:
A postcard, c/o Parnassus,
May one day reach me.

My Father's Business

'And if they ask you what you're going to do,
Just say, "My father's business".' Kind advice,
From hard-won pride: I memorised the phrase.
The school gave me, though not for that, a place.

It seemed a fiction: shambling trolleybuses
In Charterhouse Street's perennial peopled gloom,
The brave new *Mirror* building taking shape;
Old leather chairs, a dark partitioned room,

Black bulbous phones, perpetual calendars,
A working space contained and carpeted.
I'd have liked to meet his cronies in The Mitre,
But was too young. We lunched at The Globe instead.

My father had skate: I watched him closely.
His needs – fish, beer, the business – were precise:
In charge, as I am now, of a chosen world,
He gained an unsuspected gentle ease.

'Very nice.' He paid. Then back to the office:
The stairwell drenched in underwater light,
Diagonal gilt lettering on glass,
And distant steps of other business feet.

His co-director, stately and severe,
Behind a frosted door, Miss Warmington,
Who had no first name or other existence,
Fulfilled some secret, necessary function.

Across the corridor, the showroom glowed:
Glass lit through glass, a churchlike radiance,
Refracting samples of a crystal world.
One day it would all be mine? No chance.

I couldn't play the boss's son. I'd phone,
Irresolutely, Holborn 9622.
'Would you put me through to Mr Powell?'
'Who's calling?' 'Er, it's Neil.' 'Neil who?'

I could have told them then it wouldn't do.

The Dry-Cleaner's Son

The dry-cleaner's son is ruining my life.
Two years ago, he'd help out Saturdays,
Slight boyish chores rewarded with ice-cream.

Last summer he'd grown lanky, self-aware:
Out in the street, washing his father's van,
They staged a grand balletic water-fight.

Now, taller of the two, he calls me 'mate',
Will deputise for dad, or join him in
A loose bravado, male confederacy.

His shirts – today, gigantic hippie flowers –
Are as loud as his crotch-line; and his former selves
Lost postcards from the summers left behind.

You've Changed

S.L., 1990

I looked, of course, across a crowded bar,
Admired at once the perfect sense of poise,
Deep chestnut eyes, abruptly squared-off jaw
Which made you so much more than pretty. Days

Passed uncounted, months, and maybe years
Until that Sunday evening when I saw
You sitting at a table in the garden,
Dalton's Weekly and a drink beside you.

'You look like something out of Graham Greene,'
I said absurdly, meaning I suppose
You had the air of an expatriate.
I might have put it otherwise: 'You've changed.'

Immeasurable the distance that can pass
Across a glass, and then another glass:
The truths and reckless confidence exchanged
As a long evening grows to over-late.

No real surprise to see the cracks appear.
We knew them all along: the tear, the scar
Which makes us so much more than perfect, through
A lifetime spent on books and booze and boys,

On things that were, or even things that are.

In Another Light

Not even sun's false innocence
Can cover this: smaller today,
The island finds its boundaries,
Flexes as the tide subsides
And waves bathe other surfaces.

I share the land's astonishment
At the beach's lowered profile:
Planed to pebble-smoothness,
Uneasy in its changed shape,
It mutters, rattles, settles.

Gulls discover new salt lakes
Among the silent, stoic cows;
Beyond the damp seaweedy sand
Which marks the ocean's last advance,
The shingle ridge has rolled inland.

The surge spent, in another light
Storm dwindles into memory,
And children from the local school
Scatter the debris of the night,
Revising their geography.

The Stones on Thorpeness Beach

for Guy Gladwell

O luminosity of chance!
Light spins among the spider-plants
As sand or amber glow seeps through
Tall windows of a studio,
While on the beach in random rows
The enigmatic stones compose
A silent staveless variation,
The music of regeneration.

Re-learn astonishment, and see
Where splinters of eternity
Still glitter at the water's edge,
Beyond the tideline's daily dredge
Of flotsam: plants and creatures who'd
Survive this stale decaying world,
And stones worn smooth as solid tears,
Each crafted by a million years.

Or dusky rain across the sea,
Dull pewter light, when suddenly
The level sun breaks through, makes clear
Another perfect hemisphere:
Its rainbow-self, supported by
A dark horizon, arcs the sky.
I watch the colours falter and,
Slipping on shingle, fall on sand.

Yet, high above the crumbling cliff,
A concrete pill-box stands as if
In crazy gesture of defence;
As if the huge indifference
Of change, decay, might somehow be
Perturbed by such small dignity
Which slowly shifts and cracks, and so
Will shatter on the stones below.

Search for a sound hypothesis:
'Safe as houses', 'Bank on this',
Dead clichés of security!
Houses? Bank? You'd better tie
Mementoes in a plastic bag,
Chuck in the sea, mark with a flag
The spot where fish or mermen may,
With luck, remember you some day.

Our rented time is running out,
But unlike tide won't turn about
With regular and prompt dispatch
To land upon the beach fresh catch,
As gradually, with gathering pace,
Life ebbs out from the human race
Inhabiting a world grown ill.
Time for a benediction still:

Peace to the gulls and guillemots,
To curlews and their bleak mudflats,
To sea-birds, sea-anemones,
To marsh-plants, meadow-butterflies,
To lavender and gorse and mallows,
To creatures of the depths and shallows;
Peace to the vast blue out-of-reach,
Peace to the stones on Thorpeness Beach.

The End of Summer

I close my eyes. There's a knotty apple-tree,
Grasped to a landscaped lawn, its fruit unripe;
A labrador, greying at the jowls, asleep;
My mother, gently stabbing at the crossword
With mild success; my father is at work.

I am at home now, but not for long.
My imagination is going to take me away.
Things are about to change: I've heard rumours,
Like odd creaks on the stairs, while I'm in bed
Fading in tune with Radio Luxembourg.

We've been to get my new school uniform
At the outfitters: a sombre narrow shop,
Innocent of daylight or fresh air,
With a sombre narrow man who peered at me
As if I wasn't quite their class of boy.

'Still in short trousers' means just what it says:
'Only rough boys wear jeans.' Long trousers now;
My mother sews in Cash's woven name-tapes
While I watch *Juke Box Jury*. Ding! A hit!
I've seen the future and he's called Craig Douglas.

I pass whole days in an ecstasy of growing,
This wonderful summer: I empathise with plants –
Beans running, bamboo shooting, even the bees
Have somehow heard a buzz and are on the scent.
I know more than could possibly be good for me.

The stillness of held breath is on the air,
While thunder gathers in the wings of autumn.
I know high cloud will slowly bleach the sky,
Leaves turn to russet, late apples ripen,
And light will never be quite like this again.

A Virus

The words won't scan. Initials, acronyms
Are tidier though no less threatening:
They claim it for bureaucracy, as if
Depriving it of an imaginary life.

I try: I sense it crazily adrift
On a wild surge of involuntary current,
Like the lost boat in a forgotten nursery rhyme.
It had no choice in the matter, meant no harm.

But see how it turns our calm world upside-down!
Your comical pill-popping hypochondria
Seems mere rehearsal for reality,
Your lithe past an irrational vanity.

So now your boast is: 'Look, I've put on weight.'
Your breakfasting on booze has given way
To healthy muesli, yoghourt, wholemeal bread,
Storing up strength for the wasted days ahead.

Providence

The Providence Baptist Chapel, Aldringham,
Is light industrial: factory for souls,
Abandoned among heather, fern, and gorse,
Where birches lean their leaves against the wind,
It prompts old questions. Why here? Why at all?
I half-admire that monstrous confidence,
Unthinking certainty of doing good,
Which dumped a bumptious bright-red pantiled barn
Out here, far from community and road.
Now broken-windowed, boarded and patrolled
(It says) by ghostly guard-dogs, Providence
Has fallen out of use.
                                    Young oaks surprise
And jostle through the rusted graveyard fence.
The loyal congregation, being dead –
Adah Cadey, Sam Studd, Jabez Bird –
Worship in green, while yellow daisies dance
Upon the grave of Percy Marjoram,
Tended with love's defiance.
                                    I walk on,
Along a sandy track, a silent lane:
New planting, like a wartime cemetery
Or rockets poised for launch on Guy Fawkes' Night,
Proclaims the future forest's greener hope;
And a neat brick row of charitable homes
Shows how goodwill can be inhabited
As peace of mind, as warmth.
                                    Yet faith runs cold.
A sign outside the Baptist Chapel said:
Black Horse Agencies (Subject to Contract) SOLD.

Aubergines

After hours, off-duty, the young chef talks:
He perches, in his denim earnestness,
On a bar-stool, folds himself like an omelette,
And worries about his troubles with aubergines.

There are times to be not a fly on the wall,
Nor in the soup, but a kind ironic god:
Invisible, I watch the two of you press on
Through the whole ratatouille of emotion.

The Reasonable Shore

> Their understanding
> Begins to swell, and the approaching tide
> Will shortly fill the reasonable shore,
> That now lies foul and muddy.
>
> Shakespeare: *The Tempest*

And there are days, beyond dog-days of summer,
When the restless ocean gathers in repose,
Soughing and lapping at unprinted sand,
Proving that greatest power is power contained.

Shakespeare's shore of reason was the mind
Which, he believed, the tide would cleanse and fill
With water's bright lucidity. How could
A dark intelligence hold such faith in good?

The mirror-sea, example and reproach,
In each return confounds the cankered past
And leaves a world renewed with each withdrawal
(Though that is not what Shakespeare meant at all).

Sixpence for the Man

Two silver coins in penny-farthing scale:
'Half a crown, and sixpence for the man.'
Leon Molin: front, a chemist's shop.
The room beyond seemed subterranean:
Oblique light from a garden, fishtank, green.

The sharp, specific foreignness of things:
Floor-standing ashtrays, chromium-plated shrubs
With hungry bulbous roots; bright flasks of 'spray';
Loose stacks of *Titbits, Picture Post, Reveille*;
A hatstand with more coats than customers.

Waiting my turn, I'd try to calculate
Which one I'd get: the white-haired on the left,
A kindly grandfather I'd never known,
Or the smart schoolmasterly bully on the right,
Glancing at me archly: 'Next, young man!'

At home my father sometimes washed my hair
In glutinous amber shampoo: 'Soup!' he'd call,
As my dripping scalp emerged from its solution
Of Nucta Oil, brand from the gullible past,
Like Kolynos toothpaste, verdant chlorophyll –

Obtainable, no doubt, from Leon Molin.
Yet I'll retain my vexed embarrassment
At one shy boy's charade of confidence,
And two old barbers, threatening and mild,
Meekly accepting pennies from a child.

Moving House

'This is a dream,' I tell myself, waking,
'And what it says isn't real.' But there's my house,
Its stairs and its ramshackle rooms overflowing
With people from the street, and that blonde girl you knew.

I've really no idea what they're all doing there,
This whole vacant parade of the unwanted world.
Now we've found our own space, so I no longer care:
Released from your wrapping, you are my present.

Yet what subtle adjustments we've made since we began
To know each other last winter: I've even grown to love
Those dead flattened vowels you claim as Australian.
Holding you now, I could tear you apart like bread.

My head on your musky chest, I must have slept,
Waking to find the house still crowded, its furniture
Dispersed and rearranged, all out of place except
You, warm in weak sunlight on your nest of denim.

I cautiously explore: a pine table from the kitchen
Is wedged into the study, whose papers and books
Are strewn in the bathroom, my history rewritten
By strangers who view me with unconcerned reserve.

And here's the blonde girl, perched on the landing,
Leaning on a sideboard I've never seen before.
'I told you he wasn't like that,' she says, smiling.
'Oh, but' – I'm smiling too – 'he is. He is.'

Borodins and Vodka

for Dmitri Shebalin

A resident quartet.
A form of words, and yet
Through catastrophic days
This bleak eroded coast
Provides, as it has done
Before, safe anchorage.
Resident: at worst,
Administrative fiction;
At best, true habitation,
Huge vodkas in the Keys.

There's something in the air
Of Suffolk-Russian kinship:
How many programmes pair
Britten-Shostakovich.
And Ben's interpreters:
Richter, Rostropovich.
A chill from the sea, perhaps;
The windy never-stillness
Impels us to create
Our best, our better-than.

Evenings we'll not forget:
That January storm
Percussed the Maltings roof
(Tchaikovsky 3 beneath);
Fine Easter miniatures
Or summer Russian masters
With family connections
In eloquent sonatas;
A form of words, and yet
A resident quartet.

For Music

1

It's a genuine sense of my own unworthiness
that's made me delay this thank-you letter for so long,
    and still I feel nervous about beginning,
        as if our steady affair is less

a relationship than a consequence of being –
born in misunderstanding, like all biographies –
    or else an intrusion on family ties
        too intimate and too far-reaching

for me to tangle with. Your shadier relatives,
encountered long ago, in strange and shady places,
    mustn't be denied their proletarian graces
        which may, after all, have shaped our lives:

like tough boys in the playground, whose threats were promises,
they tattooed their names on a child's imagination –
    Paul Anka, Elvis Presley, Frankie Lymon
        and (O brave new word) The Teenagers –

so much packed in the emblems of a generation,
such confidence that we were the first who'd ever heard,
    that soon we'd even swoon over Cliff Richard.
        No doubt it's a shaming admission

if I confess I never liked the stuff but wanted
(as with film-stars, footballers) to have one of my own,
    or get in on the act myself. Thus began
        the world's worst pop group, and thus ended:

no harm in that, beyond embarrassment and broken
guitar-strings; as painless a way as we could manage
    to skid through adolescent rites of passage,
        though clearly it couldn't last. By then,

I'd fallen for jazz, that potent echo of an age
just past, experience just missed, yet surviving
      for the dusty, smoky moment: hours browsing
            in Dobell's basement among vintage

78s, and enraptured evenings listening
to visiting Americans, Monk or Ellington
      playing 'Round Midnight' or 'In a Mellotone'
            live in London – it don't mean a thing

if it ain't got that swing . . . Would you believe I even
wrote a monthly column for the *Daily Telegraph*
      as a 'Young Critic': took it on for a laugh,
            the records, and for Philip Larkin,

who did their proper reviews and so chose my stuff –
a kindly, sad man I'm glad in the end to have met.
      Meanwhile, formed almost the world's worst jazz quartet,
            proved that devotion isn't enough,

despite Pee Wee Thornton on alto and clarinet
(the John Coltrane of Hunter's Hill), and two more cronies
      stretched past the limit of their abilities;
            Tirez (however) *le pianiste!*

You see, Music, I'd a simple trick to learn, which is:
work at your second love, and keep your first well guarded;
      that's why I'm hunched over this sort of keyboard
            and not the illusive ivories.

2

I owe a surprising debt to Mr Collingwood,
who taught some odds and ends of English to the sixth form:
      one dozy afternoon in the autumn term,
            finding his class strangely depleted

by illness or excursion, he took the remnants home
to his flat across the High Street, bribed us with coffee,
      played a record of the Orchestral Suite in B
            minor by Bach. It worked like a charm,

works still (for heaven's sake): it's strange how momentously
the certainty struck that this was the stuff after all,
      and that it was almost inexhaustible,
            centuries of it stored up for me.

The road to Damascus? Well, nearly. Unlike St Paul,
what I'd tumbled to was addition, not conversion:
      for this was the mid-sixties, spinning on
            the kaleidoscopic musical

merry-go-round that drove the Beatles' revolution,
though it had hardly started. True, they'd topped the charts and
      even been taken seriously, had earned
            famous praise from the *Times'* William Mann

while delirious Beatlemania swept the land,
but so much of the best was still to come: *Revolver*,
      'Penny Lane' and 'Strawberry Fields Forever';
            Sgt Pepper's Lonely Hearts Club Band.

Thus some gullible critics began to consider
a grand reunion of your scattered family,
      including the freaks, all living happily
            in peace, brotherhood, etcetera;

so Maxwell Davies arranged McCartney's 'Yesterday'
(as if it needed it), and there was David Bedford
      hopping between the Soft Machine and the Third,
            and The Who with a piece called *Tommy*,

which they claimed was 'rock opera', and nobody laughed.
But meanwhile your poor relations were breeding again,
      poorer, meaner than ever, punkishly vain,
            leaving the sixties gratefully dead.

3

My formative Bach was pre-authentic: Menuhin
in boxy suites with the Bath Festival Orchestra,
        or with George Malcolm in the odd sonata;
            the Pears / King's College *St John Passion*;

and astonishing bargains – Harry Newstone's Saga
LPs of the *Brandenburgs*, Martin Galling's *Goldberg
        Variations*, ubiquitous Wurttemberg
            Chamber Orchestra, Segovia

and Rosalyn Tureck on a blurred ten-bob bootleg.
Sturdy, eternal vinyl, they travelled beside me
        through nomadic student days to provide me
            with pleasure and a musical peg

to hang my ideals on when the world rocked too wildly.
Hence the harsh injunction to descend a semitone,
        to relish scrapes and scratches of a hard-won
            warts-and-all originality

didn't seem an unfettered blessing nor was it one:
for Harnoncourt and Hogwood and Parrott and Pinnock
        (the latter in that ludicrous rustic smock)
            brought restoration, revelation,

heightened contrasts as a protecting veil was thrown back;
yet the result was uncomfortable, like living
        in a freshly spring-cleaned room, somehow wanting
            to turn down the contrast, smudge the black

and glacial white. I remember disagreeing
about not Bach but *Dido and Aeneas*, damned by
        choosing Janet Baker, not Emma Kirkby,
            unrepentant and unrepenting.

4

It's sad that certainties fell so unhelpfully
out of favour (on Radio 3 some smug buffoon
        just now said: 'No one believes in the canon
            any more'), for self-evidently

Dido and Aeneas makes an excellent touchstone:
whichever way we cast our vote, we'll have to admit
        that our desert island must have room for it,
            and that uncommitted abstention

would be unforgivable. Music, it's your habit
to make us disputatious: think how passionately
        I'll argue the merits of Gerald Finzi,
            Samuel Barber, Michael Tippett,

the off-centre romantics true to our century;
or how ruthlessly deride my cranky aversions,
        Brahms, Chopin, Liszt. Such harmless diversions
            clutter the central issue, namely

you've provided some transmogrifying occasions –
the first encounters with Shostakovich or Britten
        or Mahler, composers who've somehow grown
            to become components, possessions,

bits of the inmost self. 'And if you could take just one?'
(Whatever, you'd grow to loathe it, the question's crazy.)
        Well, it has to be Mahler, it has to be
            Simon Rattle, his Resurrection.

5

Out here in East Anglia, we're in a sense lucky:
we've one of the loveliest concert halls in the land
        (though some of the dimmest audiences) and
            the power of chance or destiny

111

has blessed it. Between works, between August storms, to stand,
as liquid-patterned starlings flock above the reed-beds,
            against the dusk, as distant lightning recedes
                    over the dark sea, and as inland

a clearing evening sky turns luminous blue and floods
the landscape with unearthly brilliance . . . this, Music,
            is beyond even your transforming magic,
                    though comprehended in your concords.

But if that conceit's a shade Pythagorean, take
a different meshing of art and geography:
            in Britten I always hear the howling sea,
                    its intermittent calm and sharp break

over the stony ridge; and it's there, obsessively,
not just in *Peter Grimes*, but a constant shifting ground
            (no paradox to those who live within sound
                    of Aldeburgh beach); inevitably,

in the intricate transactions of tides, shingle, sand,
there's a music perpetually changing, renewing.
            So now a disc of Pogorelich playing
                    early Haydn, making it new-found,

as it always is and must be, nudges at something
we might have guessed all along: that to rediscover
            is the only true discovery, that our
                    necessary task is remaking

the fractured past. In dislocated times, whenever
our lives are uncertain and our best words meaningless,
            you nourish us with coherence and wholeness:
                    Music, may you flourish for ever.

Two Rollerskaters in Oakley Square

Like evening gnats these adolescents find
        An island of late sunlight
To turn and circle in, and to unwind
        Their tangled day to night.

The dark plump one makes his agility
        Appear a conjuring trick:
A purple sphere, it's marvellous that he
        Can twist and spin and flick

His ankles over pavement-edge or grating;
        Ends vindicate his means.
Beyond, his friend comes, slyly hesitating
        In faded sawn-off jeans,

Bleached spiky hair, precisely ripened tan,
        Wide-striding sinewy grace:
He wears his body almost like a man,
        Choosing new movements, new pace.

Outing

Who's leading the procession, then?
Peter Pears and Baron Britten,
Freddy Ashton, Wystan Hugh
Auden and Herr Issyvoo,
E.M. Forster, E.F. Benson,
Angus Stewart, Angus Wilson,
John Gielgud, Joe Ackerley,
Peter Ilyich Tchaikovsky,

Patrick Proctor, Derek Jarman,
Michael Leonard, Michael Cashman,
David Leavitt, David Hockney,
David Rees, Paul Gambacinni,
Peter Tatchell, Peter Burton,
Boy outside without a shirt on
(Wishful thinking), Andy Bell,
Neil Tennant, Jimmy Sommerville,
Francis Poulenc, Edward Lucie-
Smith, Pier Paolo Pasolini,
Stephen Gilbert, Samuel Barber,
Peter Robins, Adam Mars-Bar,
Duncan Campbell, Jason who?
(Not *that* one, he'd only sue),
Desmond Hogan, Ian Charleson,
Marc Almond, er-Tom Robinson,
Thom Gunn, John Ash, Ian McKellen,
Alan Hollinghurst, Ned Sherrin,
Nick de Jongh, Chris Smith, Ray Gosling,
Matthew Parris, Francis King,
Kit Marlowe though alas Shakespeare
Wasn't *absolutely* queer,
Jeremy Beadle, Jeremy
Reed, Jules Clary, Tennessee
Williams, Oscar Wilde, Rock Hudson,
Michael Mason, Michael Nelson,
Nelson's chef Shane, Noel Coward,
Philip Ridley, Frankie Howerd,
James Baldwin, Kirkup, Dean, just James . . .
Enough of regimented names.
That wasn't too exciting, was it?
None of them is in the closet.

Yaxley

Last time here, I'd have been too small to walk,
When Freddy displayed his derelict retreat,
The Old School House (now renamed after him);
My grandmother, his devoted Tiggywinkle,
Benignly at ease in the big sloping fields.

And I can see why he'd have liked the place,
How the ancestral village touched his puritan soul;
While the vast airy spaces spoke of liberation,
His thatched hedgy corner offered sanctuary.
He craved, like all great artists, a modest nest.

Yet what am I doing, with notebook and camera,
Expecting the terror of dim recognition?
A trackless bridge, cow-parsley, distant traffic,
Cemented parish pump . . . but, beyond all this,
A scent on the air of the summer still to come.

Compost

in memory of Roy Fuller 1912–1991

The aged poet prods his compost-heap,
Reminded of a former jest that he
Might make a decent mulch eventually,
For as you sow (he thinks) so shall you reap.
He wonders at the odd longevity
Not just of turnip, say, or cabbage-stalk,
But of hydrangea's mop-head levity.
A robin watches from his garden-fork,
With sly ironic glance, who seemingly
Approves and even shares the poet's mood,
Or humours him as harbinger of food.
The other thinks of how unerringly
All compost turns afresh, on its own terms,
To flower and fruit; to poets, robins, worms.

After the Tempest

You know I always loathed the gang of them.
Two days at sea, already quarrelsome,
They squabble over titles, territory,
As if that mattered: their minds mutiny.
Meanwhile at least a kindly wind assists us;
The sky, as brittle-sharp as Venice glass,
Is cloudless; and the low late-autumn sun
Patterns the deck with shadow. An old man,
I sit here writing, unmissed, undisturbed
And (I confess) not wholly discontented:
My life at last's resolved, my long task ended,
As from the start I'd cunningly intended.
Strange, all the same, this interrupted cruise

To win back what I hadn't grieved to lose
And shan't know what to do with when we reach
The thriving port and populated beach:
An old world full of cares, affairs of state.
The point of islands is to isolate.

But there's my daughter: thinks she's royalty,
Looks forward to it, even may enjoy
A life of plots and power, of bugs and spies,
Grand gestures and expensive ceremonies.
I wish her well: or hope that food and wine
May recompense her for the asinine
Attentions of ambassadors and princes,
Bewigged buffoons and daisy-headed dunces.
Some have a taste for politics; but some
(Alas, such as myself) are overcome
By an urge to find in words the hint of meaning,
Whereas the courtly crew use them for preening –
The clause a comb, the phrase a powder-puff –
To prettify thin air, give form to fluff.

Of course, I could have stayed. You think so? No.
Not just because an end's ordained, although
It fell together like a perfect cadence,
But more because I'd outworn that pretence.
A man can't live surrounded by his errors:
I tried to civilise, to tame the terrors
Of things by nature nurtureless, untamed;
Where even sun and moon had been unnamed,
And every word rebounded as a curse,
As bad as courtly flummery, or worse!

There's no solution, then: maybe that's why,
Out here between dark sea and fading sky,
I feel this strange suspended happiness:
Things may go wrong, but things are more or less
For once beyond my meddlesome requests.
So, no more island shipwrecks, no more tempests.
When I get 'home', I'll treat the eye and ear,

Catch up with Caravaggio, and hear
What Monteverdi's written in my absence:
Who knows, perhaps there'll be a new Renaissance.
I've much to learn, and much more to forget
In my long autumn afternoon; and yet . . .

Before I lost my art, I saw the future:
How greed would feed on greed, and war on war;
Though man may learn to conquer pain, disease
Will deviously mutate. So death or madness
Must overtake the race, the failing planet.
And, worse, I came to see that this was right,
The globe's sole hope of greenness and rebirth,
Replenishing a grey, smoke-shrouded earth.
No states to govern, none to educate:
Do birds imagine? Butterflies create?
They are their art: have no need to invent
These foolish forms through which we represent
Our second-bestness. You of course will know
All this already, knew it long ago,
And yet . . . I almost said 'One last command',
Forgetting that I'd left you on our island.
The dusk draws on: I'm talking to the stars.
Perhaps, my absent friend, I always was.

Hundred River

in memory of Adam Johnson 1965–1993

We came to Hundred River through a slow October,
    when earth is scented with everybody's past;
when late scabbed blackberries harden into devil's scars,
    untasted apples rot to bitter toffee.

Across reed-beds a track of blackened railway-sleepers,
    a plank-bridge lapped by barely-stirring water;
swans gargling silently in their fine indifference;
    above, a sky of urgent discursive geese.

Now the year has turned again and I am alone here,
    where willow-herb's dry white whiskers drift over
the brick-red spikes of sorrel and the gossiping reeds;
    and the river sullen, muddied after rain.

No movement in the woods but stealthy growth of fungus,
    hesitant leaf-drop, distant scuttle of deer:
in one marbled, stained oak-leaf I sense gigantic change,
    and in the drizzle feel the season fracture.

Celandines

Some places stay for ever. Celandines
In bright rapacious grace beside the brook;
Mossed scent of earthy paths in bluebell woods;
Animal warmth of cloying straw-floored yards;
Deep meadows in their unwilled distances.

I'd play my game of hide-and-seek with life,
And win at every turn: they'd not catch me.
The garden-end and tunnelled undergrowth,
The roped and laddered oak – fine strategies
For a duke self-exiled from his childish court.

But hostile powers – Mynthurst, Stumblehole –
Defined themselves with cattle-grids or wires,
First iron curtains of the growing world:
The pebbled lane led on to tarmacked road,
Where bus-lamps shone in puddles after school.

Myself, I'd keep a life in walking distance,
Celandine-bright, mapped as a private planet.
In dreams, I'm in that other garden still:
Beyond the ditch, the fields remain unbounded,
But outer space begins at Norwood Hill.

Shell

I am schooled in the varieties of madness.
Feared beyond nickname, the Reverend dispensed
Lines for transcribing in copybook script,
Unflinching authority, Latin and caning,
As if his future depended upon it.

Borrowed on odd days, like the pitches,
With crinkle-cut hair and sandpapered face,
The games-master cultivated his own pleasures.
'Posture!' he'd yell: frozen already, we'd freeze.
On the way back to school, he'd de-bag stragglers.

After two years, we trekked upstairs to 'Shell':
A whiskery, tweedy, leathery sort of place
With squeaky hinged seats, a tuckshop cupboard,
An air of dim complicity. From Mr Salmon,
I learned only to evade his hand-picked attention.

There are photos to prove it. In one I'm slouched
Like a doll who's yet to have stuffing knocked in;
But later – I'm standing now, behind the Reverend –
There's that horrible confident smirk of survival:
I'd known most of the worst of the world by ten.

Old fools, the lot of them, not even doing
A quarter of their best, not caring or seeing
How much there was to give or how to give it;
Teaching instead bad habits by default –
Slow lessons in obsession, terror, guilt.

Road

for Nick Ash

Surely we've been here before. That road's
Strangely familiar, though the light has changed.
The echo's muted, like a song transposed.

That wayside scrub, in which so recently
Our hero planned his golden future, seems
Terminally autumnal, out of date;

And soon a pick-up truck or passing car
Will hungrily, rustily, splutter into shot,
Pass or pick up – it all depends – or not.

Above, beyond, a jagged high horizon
Shudders in haze: there's nothing much up there
But boulders, crags, sour scrags of vegetation,

A distant hint of empty winding track.
You know the line: 'This road will never end.'
Cue music. Roll end credits. Fade to black.

A Halfway House

Etched into dusk, it shows we're almost there:
Those lidded windows, biscuit-stucco walls
Between the water-meadows and the sea
Signal exact abandonment. Years drift:
Spring tides engulf it, lapping at the sills;
Gulls claim an apex among missing slates,
Shout their possession from the staring rafters;
Awash all winter, yet on summer nights
The beach will grow through shingle into sand
And turn this place inland.
                    A halfway life
May teach regard for this enduring ruin,
Weathered defender of uncertain ground,
And milestone marking that consoling point
Of nearing home, or starting out again.